SMUGGLERS, INC.
REVISED EDITION

SHAWN PARDAZI

https://www.MyLETraining.com

Cover design by Shawn Pardazi

ISBN: 979-8-218-27235-7 (print)

ISBN: 979-8-218-27236-4 (ebook)

Library of Congress Control Number: 2023916483

CONTENTS

Introduction

You've read the headlines...

"Arkansas State Police Arrest Man On I-40 With 27 Pounds of Heroin" ...

"Ohio Man Arrested by Texas Troopers With $1,230,000 in Drug Money" ...

"Teenager Caught at the Port of Entry in Laredo with over 300 Pounds of Cocaine" ...

And on it goes.

We see this type of headline almost daily when we scroll through social media or watch the news. For all except the criminals, when we see headlines like this, we wonder how this happened. For the criminals, it's a search for countermeasures and how to prevent being caught, as those featured in these articles. So yes, as the law-abiding citizens, law enforcement officers, and human beings that comprise most of the world's population, we are intrigued and hungry to know the details. This book will satisfy your hunger! But what about the criminal? Will it help their countermeasures? With 100% certainty, I can tell them that not only will they be disappointed, but the walls will close on them faster. The sheer paranoia will have its effects on their soul!

I'VE BEEN CHASING SMUGGLERS FOR NEARLY A QUARTER CENTURY

By now, you are wondering: "Who is this guy writing this book?" As a reader, I always want to know if the person writing has lived the events and speaks from personal experience, or is the person repeating hearsay nonsense and cranking out a book hoping to benefit from social engineering techniques? The reality is that I've been chasing smugglers for just about a quarter century at the time of publishing this book in December 2019. We're referred to as *Interdiction Officers* in the law enforcement realm. In my tenure, I've learned through trial and error; I've battled the concepts in court and on the road dealing with the folks I'm about to tell you about.

I hope to pass along some of the things I've learned and discovered in my work to not only help you understand what's behind those headlines, but it's also my way of helping those who come after me and will continue the mission of identifying and apprehending the smugglers. I will use stories about my trial and error to help you understand the complexity and dynamic nature of catching smugglers, not as a self-boasting measure of my abilities, but to use factual events to explain specific points. There are others doing this job who are just as capable, if not better, but they don't openly discuss their success in public or a classroom. The most successful are the silent ones, who are unknown and wish to remain that way. Most importantly, as a widowed father of a four-year-old boy and the fact that I'm nearly a half-century old, this is my way of making sure he has a bright future. He can also read this book later on in life and know that as a Middle Easterner, he can and will be able to contribute to this great nation we call the United States of America. We are a nation of immigrants, and we all must do our part to maintain its security, safety, and humanity.

My name is Shawn Pardazi! Well, not really; that's just what I go by! Living in the southern part of the United States comes with its own challenges, and if you have one of those funny names, like I do, you kind of "stick out." In some parts, that isn't a good thing! While I was born in Texas back in the early 70s to Persian parents, I went back with my mom to Iran when I was two months old until I was 15. Yes, my momma took me back because she had to go back and take care of my grandpa. It's a cultural thing because she was the oldest of the siblings, and the responsibility falls on the oldest. Now, let's be clear here. I was born in Texas, so I'm a Texan, and there's no denying that! Ha! So, get ready because this will be a no-nonsense publication full of real words, real stories, and real talk that will take you to the next level of understanding. I say this as I wear my Shemagh (Middle Eastern Headgear), listening to George Strait, toking on hookah, while I write this at this very moment. Haha!

Growing up in Iran was very interesting. I mean, who wants to be awakened at 2 a.m. with sirens going off and electricity being cut off because Saddam's MIGs were incoming and they were planning on bombing something? Esfahan, Iran is where I grew up. A typical Middle Eastern dark-skinned kid (I like to call it a natural tan) playing football (Y'all call it soccer here!) in the streets. English wasn't even an option, so by the time I came to the USA at the age of 15, I didn't have a clue how to speak English although I knew how to say five sentences my mom taught me so that I could communicate with the KLM flight attendants during my travels.

The few sentences?

"Hello!"

"How are you?"

"Very well, thank you!"

"I am thirsty and would like Coke, please!"

"Chicken," and finally,

"Where's the restroom?"

That's it! That's all I knew! Then I landed at Harts-field International Airport in Atlanta on January 28th, 1987, and for the first time as a teenager, I was in

America. It wasn't until a few years later, when I saw the movie *Coming to America* with Eddie Murphy, that I realized *Akeem* and I had a lot in common! Ha! Except my first job was at *Arby's* and not *McDowells*. I did the same job, though! "When you think of trash, think of *Shaheen*!" Haha!

In 1991 I was living in Houston, Texas, and working as a restaurant manager. By this time, I had learned a few Spanish words and had developed an obvious Texan accent. I decided I wanted to join the ranks of law enforcement. Why? My next-door neighbor at the apartment complex was a Houston Police Officer named Kevin, who became one of those secret agents with the United States Secret Service. I enjoyed riding along with him and his partners when they patrolled the southwest Houston area looking for gang members. They were part of the HPD's Gang Task Force! I started riding with him when I was 18, and the rest is history. I went to the police academy in 1994 and landed a job in a small town in Central Texas, where, after going to an interdiction class (classes that teach you how to catch criminals in transit), I hit my first big load. It was five kilograms of Cocaine. WOW! I still remember the rush! I mean, a small town of 5,000 people, and what the hell was I doing? It wasn't a local guy, though. He was an Oklahoma native going from Houston to Oklahoma City but taking the backroads to avoid being detected.

THIS SPECIALIZED ASPECT OF LAW ENFORCEMENT STARTED MY JOURNEY

This specialized aspect of law enforcement started my journey. I spent thousands of dollars of my own earnings, living on Ramen Noodles most of my early career, so I could have enough money to go and learn how this "stuff" was done. Cops working in small towns at that time know the details. Most were making less than nine dollars per hour, and that included me. I was at $8.91 an hour and thought it was good pay at the time. When it came to this counter-smuggling stuff, I was just scratching the surface. I went to many classes and even drove hundreds of miles just to ride with some guys who worked on the Interstates and looked for smugglers.

I STARTED INVESTIGATING THE INTERNAL WORKINGS OF THE CARTELS

Fast forward to 2005! By this time, I was at a Task Force type agency and intercepting loads left and right. The more I did it, the more I became hungry to learn more. I went to thousands of hours of training during the first decade, and by this time, I had made hundreds of smuggling cases. I knew where I worked was just a small part of our land mass, and I started to investigate the cartels' driving force and internal workings. I mean, up until now, most training anyone attends was based on statistical data and common denominators that have been gathered over the years. Still, just as in any pattern gathering statistical data, trends eventually change.

I wanted to know more. So, I dove into building a rapport with those I caught and started to dig deeper into how they were recruited, trained, handled, and so on. It was almost as if I was working as a handler for the Central Intelligence Agency, attempting to infiltrate the most complex organizations by conducting espionage. But, as a cop, how could I do that as deeply as I wanted to? I certainly wasn't going to go undercover. That's not my cup of tea!

I Spent Hundreds of Hours Developing a Lesson Plan

So, I devised a plan to get them to tell me how each of the mules were recruited initially, and then I worked my way into asking them to explain how their drops were made. Over the next 15 years, I spent hundreds of hours debriefing my crooks and developing a lesson plan to help others. It seemed that no matter the race, gender, origin, theater of operation, or level of operation, the commonality was that they all had to operate in a clandestine manner in one form or another, which is pretty much standard and they all had to lie to appear normal. Hence, the phrase "Nothing is ever what it seems" is so fitting in this job!

CATEGORIES OF TRADECRAFT

Over the same time, I started to document these into categories to help myself and others I taught to understand that it is not the trends that make one be able to detect the smugglers, but understanding their *Tradecraft*. I mean, the monks used to smuggle cotton out of China centuries ago, using clandestine activity and cover operations. The same has been going on with any smuggling group and operation, no matter what they are smuggling and where, for thousands of years and even today, within the confines of the border of any North American country. The same Tradecraft methods are used to maintain that clandestine edge over law enforcement. In each of these applications, the folks who are transporting must lie about it. This is how the concept was born of *Understanding the Tradecraft of Clandestine Smuggling Operations* (Smugglers, Inc.®) and the *Evading Honesty® System* that are the two main trademarked courses taught by me and my crew at my company called **Global Counter-Smuggling Training Consultants, LLC**. (DBA: *Triple I Solutions*).

In this book, I will do my best to help you understand the measures taken to maintain the clandestine efforts in hopes that you, no matter what your status and position, can fully grasp the fact that those headlines are not printed because someone by accident found a load of contraband. These headlines are a direct result of the work of silent warriors out there keeping you safe and attempting to keep those smugglers' products out of your children's hands. They are specially trained and never stop learning. That includes myself as of the time I'm writing this book.

I also want to mention that this book also serves as a reminder to those who sacrifice time away from their family to master this craft to consider that they should always put family first. Trust me, I lost my wife to an illness in March of 2018, and she sacrificed so much time away from me by pushing me to become who I am today. But the time I missed with her can never be made up. Never take time for granted!

As you read this, don't think my bluntness and attitude is because I want to be noticed. I write this because I'm passionate about sharing what I have learned, and the mere adrenaline that flows through my veins while playing this chess game is one that cannot be measured. I hope my son doesn't read this book before he's at least in high school because I don't want him cursing like a sailor at ten years old! Ha!

The Consistency of Tradecraft

I thought about writing this in third person, but I don't think my passion would show as much as it will if I write it in first person. I hope that, as a reader, you don't take it as if I'm tooting my own horn! I want this book to serve as a learning tool for those who come after me and for centuries to come. Not because of any specific trends I may write about, but rather the consistency of the existence of certain tradecraft and clandestine factors that will remain in effect now and forever until the end of human life. You will find that I will be jumping back and forth from one topic to another, as well as telling you small bits and pieces of some of the cases I've made so that you may have an easier time understanding the complexity of the work.

So, here's to my attempt to share what I have learned over the last quarter century in a no-bullshit, no nonsense, and realistic manner. We live in a world that is real, and reality is what this book is all about!

Part One
Nothing Is Ever What It Seems

THE CASH COW

It was a chilly night in October of 2009, and I was in my police Tahoe, roaming around Interstate 20 in East Texas. I was in Smith County, Texas to be exact, working for one of the best sheriffs of all time named JB Smith. He's an author too! He authored a book named *Christmas Day Murders*.

Around 11 that night, I had a dispatcher riding with me, as he was interested in how I do what I do. Dispatchers don't get the full understanding of what goes on in an interdiction officer's mind. Now, as a civilian or a rookie police officer, you may not be familiar with that term, or if you are, you may have the wrong impression of what it means. The term itself is *interdiction*, which pretty much means to Intercept. It's loosely used in police work for just about any proactive measure taken where crooks are caught by conducting minor traffic stops. There's the street level, rural and county level, and then the one that focuses on the long-distance, long-haul operations that result in the identification and capture of cartel loads.

The dispatcher, Matt, couldn't wrap his head around how I could make a simple traffic stop and, fifteen minutes later, have a guy or a few folks in custody and pull ten kilos of coke out of a secret compartment that was built in the fuel tank of the car. He was hungry and wanted to ride along to watch what was going on and see if he could make sense of it.

So, with him having been in my car less than ten minutes, I see a car coming up behind me as I'm parked on the shoulder and suddenly, the car whips into the fast lane, drops speed, and coasts slowly past me. I look over and notice the car is a rental car. After working the road for many years, we get to the point that we can tell a rental car just by certain characteristics that are displayed.

Nothing is Ever What it Seems

Being a rental wasn't what caught my attention at first, after the drastic change in driving, I saw that the rental had a US Military sticker on the back glass, promoting the US Navy. Now, I'm 100% supportive of the military, but really? On a rental? I mean, if they didn't charge me an arm and two legs, I wouldn't even put gas in the damn car when I returned one. Now, let me talk about trends and clandestine stuff a bit. Remember, *nothing is ever what it seems*. Well, exactly the case here. It wasn't that it was the *support* that the renter was showing, but rather the *convincing* he or she was doing by placing that Navy sticker on the back of that car to make the whole setup look *patriotic*. Think to yourself, why would you spend money on a sticker to dress up a rental and show *patriotism*? You can be patriotic and save money. At least put it on your personal ride. You want to support the military, donate to the foundations created for good causes, don't waste money on a sticker to place on a rental, and then have to give the car back.

I look over at Matt and say: "Holy Shit, bro, we got a load right there in that rental!"

Matt, dumbfounded, looks at me and says, "What The F*&^ Dude? How the F*&^ do you know it's a rental, and how the F*&^ do you know it's loaded?"

You see, Matt had never processed that kind of data. Now, let me also tell you that cops talk a lot of trash. We call it shit-talking, which is the same as *locker room talk*. But in public, on video in contact with the public, in the presence of command staff and other non-equal persons, we keep it professional. That's just the nature of the beast. In private and around other cops and law enforcement support teams, they're more relaxed and bust each other's balls at times. Now this culture changes from place to place and region to region. We do have our own version of asshats within the ranks who are lawsuit happy, so some agencies are strict about demeanor even in the office and amongst the co-workers.

INTERDICTION TEAMS

Now, that's just regular cops. Their culture is like being an enlisted guy or gal in any branch of the military, where in the bunks and off duty, you just cut up and have fun. But, when you talk about specialized units and specifically interdiction teams, these folks are over the top, extra and downright animals. There are no other Alphas than these folks. Not even the SWAT guys. You might as well call these dudes/chicks DEVGRU or DELTA Force of uniformed patrol. DEVGRU is also the name of the world-famous SEAL Team 6, the team who blasted Osama to where he could enjoy his BBQ fire roasting. The specialized units like interdiction are animals, not because of their tactical/physical abilities, even though most are badasses and workout like there's no tomorrow, but that big-ass personality and confidence they radiate. To the point that even within the ranks, some say they're ultra-cocky! And some are, no doubt. But most are confident yet humble. They know their shit but also don't strive for attention. They are silent and very, very, very dangerous to the smugglers. These folks are true NOCs, if there ever was a thing for interdiction work.

A NOC is that loner CIA operative who does it all from A to Z, all on his own without help. If he doesn't know it, he masters it. He doesn't quit until he achieves the result. That's what some of these animals who work interdiction are. It's all in that mindset. They own *it*! Every. Single. Time! PERIOD! If they fall, they get up and go at it again, and again, and again until they win!

I grab the gear shift, slam the Tahoe in gear, and give it all she's got. We screech onto the blacktop and haul ass forward, and I see that rental, the only car ahead of us, changes lanes again. "Oh yeah, he's watching us, bro! He's mine!" I say to Matt. As I get up to 135 MPH in that brand-new Tahoe, I come close to the rental, and using my in-car computer, I run the tag through the system to get the owner's info and make sure it's not stolen. This is the same thing any cop does before stopping a car. I mean, who the hell wants to unknowingly walk up to a stolen car and get his head blown off? I sure as hell don't. So, the computer shows me that the car is a Hertz Rental, and I flip the laptop to Matt's side and say, "I freaking told you, bro! It's a damn rental. Oh, and you better not have any plans because we're about to be neck-deep in shit in a few." He looks over, stares at me, and literally has no words. He's like a kid in the biggest *Toys R Us* store for the first time. Just in awe, and even as a dispatcher, he's amazed how I knew it was a rental way before I left the shoulder.

I knocked the car down, which means I made a traffic stop on the car, for you non-Law Enforcement folks reading. I leave Matt's big ass in the front seat and turn up my in-car speaker so he can hear the conversation that is about to ensue. I walk up, get the driver out and start explaining the reason I stopped him was that he had committed a few violations.

Now, if you're a lawyer and reading this, especially a defense lawyer, you're thinking, "Ah, I got his ass, that's a *Pretextual Stop!*" Now hold your horses, counsel! I'm not the one who dressed up a rental like that. I mean, compared to the innocent renter, doesn't that seem odd to you too? I'll just leave it at that and won't even mention that even the Supreme Court says that regardless of the INTENTION for the stop, as long as it was based on a VALID reason. And let me tell ya, he admitted he committed violations, and it was all on video. So, sit down and read the rest of the book. We're not in court! Not yet, anyway! Ha!

So, as I explain the whole thing to the guy, I'll call

JC, he goes into all kinds of stories about his trip and so on, meanwhile lying his tail off. Basically, through his lies and attempts to convince me, he was clearly engaged in clandestine activity, and he sucked at responding when I put the *Evading Honesty® System* on his behind. Oh, that's the name of our other book. The book is in bookstores everywhere and teaches you how to do rapid assessment and detect lies on anyone, your spouse, girlfriend/boyfriend, kids, and even the damn car salesman who tries to rip you off.

I am the founder of **Global Counter-Smuggling Training Consultants, LLC.** (DBA: **Triple I Solution** and there are several instructors, including myself, who travel the country teaching classes on the subject matter in this book and topics like Evading Honesty®. Nonetheless, I'll be referring to that system all throughout the book but won't list all the details of the system. That system is comprehensive on its own and only a small part of the process of *Smuggler Detection*. I would suggest you read it. It may save you headaches, heartaches, and a few dollars along the way, dealing with salespeople.

The more I talked to JC, the more I saw elements of tradecraft to the point that I even asked him to search his car, and he refused. That's a right afforded to every human who walks the land within this Great Nation, and that includes the smugglers and any other asshat who commits a crime. That's fine and all, but I had this ol' trusty buddy named *Leo* riding with me every single day.

LEO

Leo, a specially trained Belgian Malinois and trained by the best of the best named Roger Abshire of *USK9 Unlimited* in Kaplan, Louisiana, was a freaking machine. This dog pranced around everywhere we went and nut-checked every person he saw. I guess he was looking for drugs, at least, that's what I would tell them. Ha! I took Leo and told his hyper self that it was time to work. If you know about Mals, you know they don't need to be told twice. They're like a three-year-old kid but hyped up on ten pounds of meth. When they go, and you're holding that leash, it's like a locomotive just went 0 to 300 MPH in less than one second. So, old asses like me will throw out a shoulder or two in the process.

Anyways, *Leo* tells the contrary and slams the side of that rental to the point that you think he was sanding down a drywall section and about to start the painting process. That poor GMC crossover! That's all I have to say about that! The good thing was that in a gym bag, on the back cargo, there was a large amount of cash. $190,000 in cash, that is! All heat sealed in food saver packaging.

Did I mention that JC had also been through SERE training and he was a SOF Operator? SOF stands for Special Operations Forces, who are trained to survive during capture. SERE is Survival, Evasion, Resistance, and Escape (SERE). All that to say, when operating in a clandestine manner, no matter how much countermeasure training is put into the operation, the two main components will never be covered up. One is the clandestine components of the operation, and the other is the old trusty human behaviors associated with deception, which we cover extensively in the *Evading Honesty®* book. "Nothing is ever what it seems," right? WRONG! By the time you finish this book, you'll be able to tell when someone is being clandestine. And if you're a smuggler, sorry about your luck. Choose another career because the cop who's reading this will simply know how to identify you! Ha!

RECRUITING AN ALL STAR

After the bust, I sat down with JC. He was in the military and was doing it for the same reason every other smuggler does it. And that was for MONEY! So, yes, that is it. It's all about the money for all of them. I'm talking about the real smugglers. Not the punk hood rats who sling dope and show off their guns and shit to look cool. I'm talking about folks who are part of complex operations. I'm talking about organizations like the Sinaloa Cartel, which was run by El Chapo Guzman, and others like the Medellin Cartel, which was founded by Pablo Escobar and his US operations that were run by Griselda Blanca during the Cocaine Cowboys Days of Miami and NYC! That kind of operation. Not some *Little Wayne* small-time dope running out of New Orleans that he raps about!

JC AND PARALLELS WITH OTHER CASES

JC came clean and even did some super-secret shit with some intelligence folks in and out of the country, and that's all I'll say about that. But, what was really cool is that he and I, along with Chris (a close friend and an interdiction officer in California) got to spend weeks together and learned all about how he was recruited, trained, and even how he worked his way up to the point that he decided how to run the loads. This was back in 2009, and as I debriefed JC over a two-year-long process and at times brought him to some classes so he could tell the officers his story, I started to see that even though he was a totally different type of smuggler, from a different background and worked for a totally different segment of the drug trafficking world, I started to draw the parallels with other cases I had made in the last 15 years with the way he maintained his clandestine approaches.

JC was recruited by the Arellano Felix Cartel, which was the cartel in charge of Tijuana, Mexico. For those of you who haven't a clue where that is, it's the huge city that is on the Mexican side of San Diego, California. The Land Port of Entry (POE) sits between these two cities, and it's called the San Isidro POE. The largest and the busiest POE in the world.

JC had been in a bar, hanging out with some military comrades, when a girl bartender that he was having relations with introduced him to a Mexican dude that was hanging out at the edge of the bar. The

Mexican guy had asked JC if he wanted to buy some blow. Blow is a slang word used for Cocaine. He had pulled about an ounce of coke from his sleeve and showed it to JC. Being a cocky dude and a special force-type military operator, JC tells the guy to go screw himself and not to be showing childish weight to him in public. The Mexican guy asks him, "What the hell are you saying about it being childish weight?" JC tells the guy that he doesn't want to see small-time dealers. Essentially, JC is talking down to the guy as if JC is a big timer in the game. Not that he was a big-timer, as he wasn't even involved. But the machismo factor is strong amongst the Special Operations Forces (SOF) guys in the military. JC ends up brushing the guy off and carries on with his drinking and playing pool with his buddies.

Two days later, the chick from the bar calls JC, "Hey, remember the guy at the bar that tried to sell you that blow?" she asks of JC.

"Yeah, what about that motherfucker?"

"Well, he's been asking me to have you call him if you want big weight to move. He says he thinks he can help you with that."

By this time, the dude is thinking JC is a smuggler and wants to do business with him. JC, being the cocky ass he is, tells the chick: "Give that motherfucker my number and tell him to call me." A few hours later, the dude calls JC and wants to meet him at the local AM/PM store. These are the typical convenience stores you find on the West Coast. They're the equivalent to the local 7-11 stores. The next day, JC meets the dude and another guy at the AM/PM, and they ask him if he's interested in moving weight.

JC said that once he was in the game and truly knew the insides, he started realizing that he was one of the prime candidates they looked for. Not necessarily JC, but his type of person. The cartel there was interested and actively recruiting younger white males to help run loads up the coast to Oregon, Washington, and the East Coast for the Tijuana Cartel.

The Tijuana Cartel, also known as the TJ cartel or the AFO (Arellano Felix Organization), was attempting to make a move into the market of New Orleans after Hurricane Katrina destroyed it and ran all the large-scale smuggling shops out of the city. The areas used to be controlled and supplied mainly by the Gulf Cartel from the TX/MX Border, but AFO had seen an opportunity to move in and take over.

THE CARTEL ACTS LIKE THE CIA

The cartel, always operating in clandestine ways, works much like the CIA and how they recruit. They recruit specific types of folks for a specific type of mission, which would be able to operate clandestinely in the open and fit in. If you think about it, there weren't many Hispanic folks living in the New Orleans area before Katrina. Sending members of the Mexican Cartel there that early would certainly look suspicious. So, the trend at the time was to hire white folks (especially military) so that it wouldn't draw attention.

I mean, we all know there are a large number of military bases along the southern region of the US border that run across the whole USA. You have the Navy in San Diego, the Marines just north of them at Camp Pendleton, then 29 Palms, the Army and Air Force bases in Arizona, New Mexico, and even Ft. Bliss in El Paso, Texas, all through San Antonio and Ft. Hood, Texas, where members of the military are always seen driving down every single interstate at any time of day or night. So, what better smuggler than one who fits the part? After all, who would suspect the military members of betraying the country?

The reality is that even though anyone can sign up for the military, it's not necessarily because of morals. Some just join because of its benefits, and they learn a trade. Nonetheless, JC was not only fitting that mold, but he was also a member of a special unit that already had learned the concept of operating under the radar and in a clandestine manner. Just not the type to be applied within the confines of the U.S.

JC Plays His Cards Right

JC tells the guy he needs time to think about it and he doesn't know them and if it's a set up. He plays his cards right. He's looking for an upper hand at this point. If he would have told them okay the first time, they would think he was weak. JC wasn't about to make it known to them that he was struggling, because then they would be in control. The struggle he spoke about was financial. As an E-5 (Enlisted 5 Series Pay Grade), at the time JC was only making around $30K a year and living in southern California. One of the most expensive places in the United States. He wasn't deployed and would not be for the rest of his enlisted time, because he had suffered an injury that would make him operationally incapable to deploy on missions.

He was placed at the main office of his assignment to basically ride his time out and retire with benefits. Without the deployment and other pay that comes along with hostile area deployment, he was having a hard time making ends meet. On top of that, he was engaged to be married a short time later. So, he was a prime candidate, no doubt, for them, and they were just what he needed at the moment.

A few days later, the chick from the bar calls JC to come to the bar, and when he goes there, she hands him a burner phone and tells him to answer it when it rings. JC leaves the bar, and within thirty minutes, he gets a call. He's told by a voice to go back to another AM/PM store and see a guy in a white GMC truck. JC drives over and no truck is to be found in the parking lot. As he's about to leave, a GMC pickup rolls in and a bald Mexican guy with tattoos nods at him to back up and park. JC backs up, pistol in his waistband and parks. The GMC pickup pulls to the opposite side of the parking lot and a black sedan pulls to the gas pumps in front of JC's car. The guy from the passenger seat of the sedan gets out, makes eye contact with the dude in the GMC truck, looks at JC, nods and walks to JC's car. He gets in the front passenger seat and gives JC an envelope. A legal-sized envelope that is. JC, not saying a word, opens the top and sees three bundles of rolled up $100 Bills, totaling $15K.

The Money Seals the Deal

The Mexican guy takes the envelope back and tells JC: "Bro, that's yours for your first run if you want it, but you have to leave tomorrow, so I need to know now." JC, already hard up for money and seeing half of his annual salary in that envelope agrees and he's told to go home and pack, but make sure not to let the burner leave his side. JC, by now pumped with adrenaline, is worried, scared, and excited. He explained it as if it was his first time jumping from a plane during his jump school in Georgia. He said he had mixed emotions, but the money was way too convincing.

JC ends up taking the offer and starts to work for these folks. Eventually, he makes runs for them about four to five times a month and averages about $30K a trip. That's about $120K to $150K a month, after all the expenses. A shitload more than what he would be making as an E-5. What was on his side was that due to injury and not being deployable, he had free reign as to scheduling.

The SOF community doesn't work like the normal military. They are called upon for special missions and when not on a deployment or a training mission, they're like any outside sales job. They have to call in to check with their command once a day but are pretty much able to do whatever they need to do privately. And since he was injured and his buddies were always gone overseas or on training missions, he was pretty much just hanging out at the base or running errands for his command or even taking trips and checking in with the phone to his Commanding Officer. The flexibility made it easy for him to make runs.

What was amazing was that he had been stopped numerous times on the way cross country by other interdiction officers, but *they never searched his car*. This was in part because he always had orders showing he was traveling for the military and always had his gear with him. His M.O. (Modus Operandi) was always the same. He would dress up the rental cars, which is all he used, and load up all his military gear in it except weapons and use the scene to gain empathy from any law enforcement that would stop him. And it worked until I stopped him.

THE CARTELS WORK LIKE THE CIA

JC's recruiting is nothing new. As mentioned, the cartels work like the CIA. Depending on their need, their recruitment targets are selected in that manner. In South Texas, where the oil industry is the main source of income and employment, most cartel organizations will recruit from within the oil field industry. They even go as far as setting up their smuggling cars to look like oil field work cars and trucks. It makes them look normal in the scheme of things locally. JC was military and not the only one who was working for the cartel. Each year, we hear of at least a few military folks being arrested for smuggling. They also fall victim to greed and good pay.

What's amazing near the border is that sometimes the cartels are able to recruit law enforcement on the USA side. We hear about the Mexican police being bought out, but the USA has its own numbers too. In the last TEN years, many local, county, state, and even federal agents like DEA and border patrol have been apprehended by the government for either running loads or facilitating smuggling operations.

A quick Google search will result in many news releases. It's an unexpected and immoral act for a law enforcement officer to get involved in smuggling, but the greed for money sometimes has a lot of control over decisions. But, to also be fair, there are exceptions to that. I have heard of a couple of cases where the border agent's family was being held as collateral for the agent to allow a load through. At that point, the agent had no choice but to preserve the lives of his relatives. But what he/she failed to do each time was to report the events to their boss. Some say they were afraid of leaks, and some don't agree. Either way, it happens, and it's part of the smuggling business. In the world of espionage, this is called human assets. They are used for the purpose of the mission and compensated well for their efforts.

JC's story isn't an anomaly at all. It rings true to the basics of how recruiting takes place. I remember back in 2005, I stopped a U-Haul truck headed from Mission, Texas, to Cicero, IL, where the driver could *possibly have a job as a mechanic*. After a few minutes of interviewing and searching the truck, I found 700 pounds of marijuana stuck in five large U-Haul boxes in the truck. No attempt was made to conceal them at all. Just furniture was all around the boxes that contained big bundles of weed.

When debriefing this fella, I learned that he had been recruited by his cousin. The reason was he had lost his job as an electrician at the *Citgo Refinery* in Corpus Christi, Texas, and his expenses far outweighed his income. His cousin wanted to help him out and set him up with a smuggling group to make money and offset the lost income. He met with a handler in a shopping area, just like JC had done, where he was told to go by the U-Haul rental location and meet a specific person to get a U-Haul Box Truck. The rest of these types of transactions and operations will be discussed in length in the chapters that follow. The common theme with almost 100% of the smugglers that I have encountered has been that they were recruited because they could be an asset, and the money was the motivation.

Some think to themselves that smugglers are all low-life, uneducated thugs with no common sense, when in reality, they are just like you and I and simply happen to have the right connections to get into that realm. The way folks are recruited can vary from meeting candidates at a workplace and seeing that they would be good assets, being related to the smugglers through family, being neighbors and growing up together, and even having spent a short time in a low-level jail with a member of the cartel, where trust could have been built during the time they had served. All in all, the cartel operates in a clandestine manner, and whatever the needs are and whoever could get the job done has the potential of being recruited. We've even had cops and federal agents join the ranks of smugglers.

THE ART OF SMUGGLING

JC was sent on his first few trips, being escorted by not only a scout car but also a protection car. A scout is a car that travels ahead of the loaded car so that it can alert the load car of any police presence ahead. This is a common occurrence for loads that originate from the Southwest border, especially for new recruits. You see, there is a time period where the new recruit is on an evaluation period, and trust has to be made. Plus, there must be some kinks that have to be worked out about certain parts of the transportation of the product.

Scouts typically attempt to get the attention and play as decoys as well if they think the load car may become a target of an officer to be stopped. Their job is to deflect any attention from the load car onto themselves, if possible. The protection car's job is to ensure that the driver of the load car doesn't just take off with the load and steal it, and/or if the car is stopped, make sure the handlers know so that measures can be taken to protect assets on both ends. Some have to do with trust at the beginning, but mainly they are there to protect the load from being stolen. They are the eyes and ears of the cartel, so to speak.

Smugglers Don't Want any Friction With the Police

Sometimes officers assume that the protection car means they will attack the police. I'm sure it has happened in the past, and we know for a fact that it happens south of the border, but smugglers in general don't want any friction between them and the police stateside. They're more concerned with the business and not interested in drawing attention to themselves. Attacking officers over a single load, when it would just be minimal loss, would not be beneficial to their operation at all. It would generate heavier scrutiny and a lot more resources being put forth to catch them, thus it's not worth the entire operation's security.

JC Devised a Plan

As time went on, AFO started to trust JC and let him run his own schedule. He was given a 4-day leeway to get to and from New Orleans on his long runs, but he devised a plan to not only get rid of the scout and protection cars, but also to build more trust. JC wasn't alone either. He said there were other military members who worked for the AFO, and there were hundreds of regular people who he had seen at the stash houses they were running. However, he wanted to control his own movements and rely on his own instincts. He thought the folks in charge of the transportation were too sloppy. For example, they wanted him to stop at certain places and get a hotel room on the way east. He thought to himself that stopping and carrying big bags in and out of a hotel room was not only too risky, it would also look suspicious. He was right too. As interdiction officers, we also work closely with hotel/motel interdiction units at times to pass on intelligence we get off traffic stops and road seizures; and they know all about suspicious activities at hotels. JC would have been a prime target for these guys/gals, if they would have seen that kind of activity.

So, JC decided to bypass the whole stopping at certain areas and came up with the idea of GPS trackers so that the AFO handlers could see where he was all the time. He even told them that he would look more legit if he drove longer hours and just pulled over to rest at a rest stop, rather than a hotel, because most military folks who travel on orders do just that to get to their destination faster. You see, JC had it figured out the whole time. Since he was in the military, he had hired a fellow soldier on the base to cut him fake travel orders. He paid the guy $2K a month to make sure he had legit orders, showing he was on a recruiting detail to wherever he was going. JC also didn't stop there, he also loaded up his car with all his military-issued gear, minus the guns, and would tell folks he was on a recruiting mission for the unit.

THE COVER STORY

Hell, that's what he told me the night I stopped him. Except, I could tell he was not quite telling the truth, and the way he explained himself, I could see he was giving me a cover story. A cover story is a component of the tradecraft used by the smugglers operating in a clandestine manner and we'll explain that later in the chapter *Non-Official Cover*. As a matter of fact, that chapter will detail some of the most revealing details of how smuggling operations work, their tradecraft, and the efforts to maintain the clandestine operational edge. But they can't pull wool over the eyes of those who specialize in detecting clandestine activities.

THE CARTEL GAVE JC POINTERS

JC sure did have his act together. As mentioned, he had been stopped a few times by interdiction officers on his trips, but they never went further than thanking him for his service in the military and letting him go with a warning. He had a good storyline in place, a set of tangible props in his car that supported his story and it made sense to officers or anyone that would ask him about his journey. He even had been put through a few scenarios in a clandestine location, where the cartel members made mock traffic stops on him and gagged his interview skills, giving him pointers on what to focus on.

He said one time, they even ran a dog on the car he was driving, during the mock traffic stop and told him how he needs to stand and what he needs to do in the event a dog was deployed by the cops. It was basically a coaching scenario that all their transporters would undergo.

The magnitude of preparation efforts that took place for the hauls was out of this world. You would think that they were running a multi-billion-dollar operation and needed to be so detailed. Oh wait, they are, and they continue to do so. What JC had to do was get the load from one place to another within a certain period of time, but after the trust had been built and the AFO cartel knew he was safe to let operate solo, they let him handle his own ways. They saw that the system he had devised worked for him and he was mastering it.

Normally, mules are given specific directions on

how to make runs, what to do at certain junctions, when to call, what routes to take, and so on. They're also given certain directions as to what to do to communicate in the event of capture, what they can and can't say. JC's case was different. He was like a contract driver. Much like the guy in the movie *Transporter*. An independent driver who is hired to drive a load from one place to another and does it his own way.

After a few months, JC became one of their most valuable drivers. He was so valuable that they would even invite him to special parties for the higher ups in Mexico and he would attend as a guest of the leaders. They even nick-named him *Rambo*. What needs to be made clear is that JC's case is not normal. The normal drivers of the load cars are given a car, told what must be done, when calls need to be made, and so on. So, don't think that all smugglers are the same. There's no standard of application. Each driver is allowed a certain level of self-generated ideas, if it fits within the operational norms of the cartel. JC type smugglers are few and far between.

SMUGGLING IS AN ART

At the end of the day, there is a ton of preparation and a complex set of dynamics that exist in the smuggling world, but it's also an art. Some of the world's best smugglers are fooling law enforcement daily throughout North America. And if they can do it so easily, what about spies and foreign nations who want to do harm to the U.S. and have clandestine operators within the U.S.? Makes you wonder what else happens behind the scenes that we don't hear about most of the time. Luckily, we have an awesome group of counter-espionage experts that keep us safe every day! And we never hear about what they do nor when they take out an attacker.

I could go on and on about the various ways the cartels have mastered this art of deception, but this book would be over 1000 pages and no one would be interested in all that reading. Not to mention, I'm doing my own audiobook and I can't talk that long. I'd rather work the road and catch another smuggler to be honest. But keep in mind, in my four-day class, I can't even cover the various ways. Truly understanding the operational components of a smuggling group would make things a lot clearer.

PILOT'S LICENSE
FOR FREE

After about two years of running loads every single month, JC thought to put himself through flight school with the money he had made. And he mentioned it to his handler, who was within the closest of the friends to the AFO leader. They agreed to help him and actually paid for all his pilot licenses. Soon, he started running loads using planes, making four to five runs to the East Coast each month. He was becoming so valuable, they started investing in him and using some of his ideas, especially the tracking by GPS on other mules they had on payroll. You have to understand that JC's position was unique, and he was creative. However, investments aren't made in everyone. The cartel operation is a business after all. Every business hires employees and some are worth investing in for better results. They become valuable assets. But at the same time, there's still a level of anonymity that goes with the whole cartel thing.

IN PLAIN SIGHT

When it came to flying, JC would file a normal flight plan, dress as if he was a businessman, and would make scheduled stops along the way for fuel. He never drew much attention to himself. He would be hauling anywhere from 300 to 600 pounds of hydroponic weed and would have it in military duffle bags in the plane and in plain sight. That was his way of hiding it. All in plain sight! The concept of "Nothing is ever what it seems!" rings so true here! Plus, he filed a flight plan each time with the FAA and never deviated from it. He made it seem normal. He never popped on anyone's radar as doing anything suspicious. That's what you call operating clandestinely!

One trip, JC had brought in about 300 pounds of weed, about 200 bottles of codeine syrup and some cocaine. He flew right into New Orleans Airport. Flying on a private jet, you don't come to the commercial gates. You go to specific executive hangers and that's where you park and unload. When he had pulled up to park the plane, he saw their US Customs and Border Protection (CBP) K9 trucks.

New Orleans Airport is an international airport and has a lot of incoming South American private jets landing there. Any international airport is considered a Port of Entry, just like the San Isidro POE mentioned and CBP Agents have jurisdiction to inspect passports, cargo, luggage, and whatever else they feel they need to check. No different than flying into any international airport from outside of the U.S. The blue uniform folks can literally search anything, including your phones, tablets, and computers for anything related to national security. So, hiding 300 pounds of weed would be a thing for them too.

JC didn't get inspected that night, but it scared him. He went about his business and dropped the load, picked up the cash and headed back the next day on his return flight. But the next trips were all destined for a smaller airport in St. John's the Baptist Air Strip, where he didn't have to worry about the CBP. Hell, he didn't have to worry about anything there. It was hardly used. He would land, make a call and the folks he was supposed to meet would show up, unload the duffle bags right off the plane into their vans and SUVs, give him the cash already packaged up and he would fly right back out. He did stop a few times in Texas and visited family along the way. No one questioned him and he had a great cover.

USING AIRPLANES DAILY

Using airplanes is not unique to JC. Airplanes have been used for many decades as a mode of smuggling. If anyone ever watched the show *Cocaine Cowboys*, you remember that the Columbians were flying their dope from South America to Miami and New York City using planes just about every day. Even the Juarez Cartel, headed by Amado Carrillo Fuentes, used planes to wholesale buy and distribute cocaine from the Medellin Cartel.

Planes are a fast and efficient mode of smuggling. The FAA estimates that more than 44,000 flights are conducted within the US airspace daily with 2.7 million folks in the air in a 24-hour cycle. Each has a flight plan electronically filed with the FAA. Now, how many folks would it take to keep track of all these flights to see the 100 or even 300 that might be smuggling? And, those numbers are just a guess. Could be more or less. Who knows? All I know is that 44,000 flights and how many sets of eyes watching and thinking? It's nearly impossible. Now think of JC. Filing a legitimate flight plan and sticking to it. Never would set off alarms. It's like a normal day at the FAA.

JC was an oddity for sure in the cartel world. A white dude, pilot's license, free reign over the air, free access to all the routes used by the cartel and even personal invites to the AFO ranches for family outings like weddings, Quinceañeras and other notable events. A Quinceañera is the 15th birthday party of a Mexican female and a very important event in the girl's life. It is celebrated by large parties and gatherings throughout Mexico and anywhere Mexicans live.

We have them stateside all the time, which itself causes issues on traffic stops. You ask how? So, it is an event that is only significant to Mexican culture. We see folks of Mexican heritage traveling days across the country to attend a Quinceañera for one day and then drive back. An extremely normal thing to do, but in the eyes of American Culture, it is the most odd and implausible travel plan. Think about that for a minute. Unless you're Mexican, it would seem odd to drive 48 hours, stay for 18 hours to attend a party and rest, then drive 48 hours back. To some it's insane and to Mexicans it's normal. I can tell you I have seen officers use that as reason to think the people were doing something wrong.

Over the course of several years, between flying and driving, JC made over 250 trips. Just the first year, he made 54, as he recalled. Think about those numbers and making $30K or more each trip! Add the numbers up. That's over $7.5 million dollars. Now compare that to the salary of a little over $30K a year as an E5 in the military! Now it should make a little more sense how that greed gets the best of some folks. We're not questioning morals here, because money can make the most moral person become immoral, if the need is there. In his case, the high cost of living in Southern California was definitely a huge contributing factor. He always said, "I don't know why the fuck they put a Navy Base and Marine base in that part of California, where you have to sell your soul to pay the rent." And that is exactly why other members of the military there are susceptible to do the same thing. And according to him, we are doing it and still are. One thing for sure, he won't give up his buddies!

NON-OFFICIAL COVER

(Smuggling Tradecraft)

For many years, even now, officers get training that focuses on common denominators to decipher through a multitude of factors, or so-called indicators, to detect smugglers. In time, I realized it wasn't ever about the common denominators that I would see physically, or the stories I tried to make sense of at roadside, but rather the stories that made total sense were filled with efforts to cover up something, what I refer to as *Clandestine Measures*.

Things like how a car was registered to hide transfers from one mule to another, how mailbox addresses from the UPS store were used to not tie the car down to a certain place and even how the cars were set up to resemble what the story was in an effort to make things look and sound legit. Even things like someone not knowing the year model and make of the car they had *just bought* and were taking a trip in it.

IT CLICKED WITH JC

Meanwhile, I look back and kick myself in the ass for letting go of so many loads from 1994 to 2009. Even though I had started to pick up on the tradecraft of clandestine operations and even was pretty good at interviewing and catching folks in lies, it wasn't until JC that it all clicked for me. It just did. The reason was that when I looked back, there were hundreds of times that I would see tradecraft components like the above-mentioned measures, but I was too caught up in whatever the trend was at that time of that specific theater of operation. Trends like focusing on a specific make of car because recent seizures around the country showed that car being used the most to haul drugs and build compartments in to hide them.

I worked a north/south road in the beginning years of my career. A road that started at the U.S./Mexico border and went all the way to the Canadian border. Of course, at the time, the targeting was focused on cars coming from or going to the border. So, I was conditioned to misinterpret what was relative to the Southwest border culture as the indicators to look at rather than what was relative to clandestine activity. By this, I mean that I focused on the rosary beads, the statues of La Santa Muerte, Jesus Malverde, and any other articles that were associated with the Southwest border culture.

All of these are physical items that are, in one way or another, only associated with Mexican Culture. The

Rosary beads are the Catholic prayer beads. Most Mexicans are Latin Catholics, so it's normal for them to have them, along with Virgin the Guadalupe pendants, statues, or even stickers on their cars. La Santa Muerte is a folk saint in Mexico, associated with groups that focus on the afterlife. It's not a recognized saint of the Catholic church, but also not only related to drug trafficking, as some may think. And Jesus Malverde is a folklore hero of the Mexican State of Sinaloa. It is said that he would steal from the rich and give to the poor. He's used as an icon for protection, the same as Santa Muerte by those traveling. Some of them also use it for protection, as they travel with loads being smuggled.

I was focused on these elements so much so that if any of that stuff wasn't there right off the bat as I stopped a car, I would let it go. But, as I matured in the job and especially between JC and a few other busts before and after him, I started to see that smuggling had a tradecraft that would vary from place to place, but it is all designed to maintain clandestine operations. This was clear when I realized working an east/west road didn't expose me to the Southwest border culture as much as it does demographics from all walks of life and many cultures. Boy, had I missed some loads!

I traveled for nearly five years in the mid-2000s. I worked alongside interdiction officers from West Texas, East Texas, Georgia, Louisiana, Mississippi, and Arizona, and even went up to the Shasta Mountain region and worked with the guys near Redding, California. What opened my eyes was that each of these areas had smugglers, but the demographics would change as the origin and destinations changed. The class of smuggler would change. The trends of the cars they used would change, and even to the point that their loads would change, based on the supply and demand of the region they were supplying.

ONLY TWO THINGS REMAINED THE SAME

Only two things always remained the same in every single one of these areas. The first thing was that anyone who is a smuggler will exhibit deceptive behaviors because they have to lie about what they are doing, and the second thing was that because of the need to have a cover story as a part of their attempt to stay clandestine, their tradecraft pointers would remain the same. The way they would register cars from one person to another or even through small mom-and-pop dealerships, addresses they would use, and many other elements that vary to some degree on every stop, but collectively are designed to create an illusion and hide the truth. Hence the term tradecraft of clandestine activity. They literally use the same techniques the CIA uses when deploying spies all over the world.

OPERATIONS ARE COMPARABLE TO LARGE SCALE DISTRIBUTION BUSINESSES

There's a misconception that all drug dealers are the same as smugglers. There is a level of operation within the drug business, and it's comparable to large-scale distribution businesses. The best way to explain it is if I was explaining how Walmart works as a corporation but also focuses on its fleet operations and its transportation of goods. Now, this is in no way saying Walmart is somehow involved in illegal activity, but I'm going to use them as the basis of how a large-scale operation conducts its business when it comes to fleet management and distribution of products.

To make it easier to understand, I'll break down the two main components of supply. There is the ordering aspect when a store submits a request for certain products to stock, and then there is the delivery part that involves a truck that will pick up and drop off the product ordered. What we have to take into consideration is that all the people involved in this large-scale operation are all Walmart employees, so there is not actual purchase or sale of product within the ordering and transportation arena, but rather just moving inventory around from warehouses to the front line, where it can be sold to a customer. So, you can imagine that the driver of the truck that takes a trailer full of toilet paper from the Walmart distribution center to the local store is not going to drop off the trailer, pick up another and a check for the toilet paper's payment and head back to the distribution center. The reason is that the entire operation is part of the Walmart program and is not reliant on sales at the internal level.

What else is important to know is that the drivers and the warehouse workers don't have any personal interest in the product they deliver, nor the product sold. They are just getting paid to facilitate the movement. The driver of the truck either gets paid by the number of miles he drives or an hourly rate, as well as the stocker and the person inside the receiving dock who operates the forklift. There's no loss at the individual level, if a Walmart load is lost due to an accident, so long as it is not the fault of the employee. At worst, if the employee was at fault and it was deemed that the employee poses too much risk at work, the employee would get fired or reassigned to another position that would carry less responsibility. Further breakdown of the transportation part of the distribution of Walmart products includes the fact that there is another larger warehouse that supplies the local distribution center, which also employs drivers. All being Walmart employees.

Now, the vehicles that are driven by the distribution staff are all corporate vehicles, registered to the company, maintained by the company, and not the responsibility of the operators. That includes the forklifts. Essentially, the operation and all its components are property of the larger corporation. When we look at the way the corporate vehicles are registered, they are all registered to the company and easily tracked down and located.

SMUGGLERS COUNTER SURVEIL THE TACTICS USED BY LAW ENFORCEMENT

Smuggling organizations operate similarly, when it comes to asset management, fleet operations, even the pay for the employees. Except, they distribute illegal things and operate in the shadows. Let's take the example of a car being used. While Walmart fleet is registered to Walmart and a legitimate address, a smuggling organization at the highest level will register the car in the name of the driver to make it appear personal. This information comes from decades of officers reporting a third-party owned car as an indicator and listing it in their reports as one of the reasons why the situation was suspicious. Smugglers use previous reports from cases to counter surveil the tactics used by law enforcement. It's a way of doing risk management if you think of it that way. They go back and study what went wrong and how they lost a load to the authorities and use those scenarios to adjust and continue to work out the details of staying out of the limelight.

I have seen the more organized outfits and larger operations go as far as having their drivers rent rooms or even apartments and use those addresses, even if they never stay there. One of the common tactics used as of the writing of this book is the use of apartment complex addresses, leaving out the apartment number.

However, the mailing address of the car's tag renewal would be another address, usually a PO Box. This way if the car in question becomes suspect and efforts are made to set up surveillance on it and follow it, it would not be parked or seen at the address listed and if it's a complex, it would lead cops to dead ends and a wild goose chase. So, you can see how these operations at every level, require some sort of tradecraft to maintain anonymity along the way. That in itself, establishes suspicion. Think of it this way, why would you as the reader go through all that trouble if you weren't trying to be sneaky? Right? So, that should show how when compared to the general public, these type tradecraft markers would be huge factors in determining clandestine activity. At the end of the day, the officer relies on these to take actions, but must also justify them in the eyes of the constitution and in court.

Levels of Operation

Now that you somewhat understand the complexity of the transportation aspect of the smuggling world, let's look at the levels of operation, but we'll also compare it to the same corporation, which is Walmart. So, if Walmart itself is the largest distributor of certain products that are carried in their stores and sold to customers, they would be considered high-level distributors, because of their size and sheer volume of sales. That also means they have more money and resources to have better planning and execution in place, a much smoother process, and a lot of support in place. Walmart trucks would deliver the goods to their local distribution center and no money would be exchanged. The product would simply go down the supply chain and eventually to the stores and on the shelves. This entire process is handled by Walmart employees. Even to the point that it is sold to the consumers. Walmart's operation mirrors a *High-Level Drug Trafficking Organization,* which we'll call a DTO from now on. The High-Level DTOs have hundreds of drivers that run to and from various stash houses (much like the Walmart distribution centers) and bring products to restock. Those stash houses then supply another distribution point as compared to a Walmart store located in a certain area and then on to direct consumers. The complexity of how they work is astonishing.

SYSTEM TO PREVENT LOSS AND PROTECT ASSETS

The High-Level DTOs have a system in place to prevent loss and to protect assets. They give the cars to the drivers and tell them to drive. The car may be in the driver's name, but the driver has no clue of the year and model or must think about it. There are payment issues with the car. When a car is given to someone to register in their name, they never paid for it, so when questioned about it, a person who is trained in detecting deception can immediately pick up on the fear-based responses. This is how the tradecraft of putting the car in the name of the driver and the behaviors that the driver exhibits when questioned about it, will allow a fully trained interdiction officer to recognize the overall big picture and be able to categorize the encounter to one that depicts clandestine activity. There are many moving parts and hundreds of small acts that are tale-tell signs of tradecraft. Those are all discussed in the ***Smugglers, Inc.*®** classroom training courses and for law enforcement only. But you should get the idea by now that none of this stuff happens by accident.

The levels go from high to mid-level, which is when a smaller DTO will connect with a larger DTO to purchase products at wholesale rates. This parallels the BBQ shop owner going to Sam's Club or Costco to buy ten briskets and cook them to sell to consumers. Or even ordering as a restaurant from McClain or Sysco Foods as a wholesale buyer of larger bulk foods. The mid-level then sells straight to the consumer.

The next level down is the low level. That would be the person who goes to Walmart, buys a carton of cigarettes at regular price and then sells single cigarettes in the neighborhood to the less fortunate. He would be the low level or street dealer. The street dealer does travel to buy his product but also comes from the street life and most likely has weapons and may attempt to protect his investment. He doesn't work for anyone and is more likely to lose if captured. So, that's where the fight or flight kicks in. Most of those who work interstates, focus on the high and mid-level to prevent the mass distribution itself.

The high level doesn't allow the driver to know where to go. They're compartmentalized for safety. They don't want to risk the supply end and the recipient end being targeted if the driver is apprehended in the middle of transporting the load. This means when the driver is asked by the interdiction officer where he's going, he won't know and will say something like "I call for directions when I get close." Sounds like some sort of military-style limited information dissemination tactic, doesn't it? It's what defines the complexity of the operation and the need for security. In the military and the CIA, it's called Operational Security or OpSec!

Elaborate and Complex Hidden Compartments

The high-level cars also have elaborate and complex hidden compartments. Who would ever think that a gas tank would be cut and only one-fourth of it used for gas and the rest filled with Cocaine? What about the same concept, but the content of the other side of the tank is liquid meth? Smugglers at this level use whatever method necessary to transport. Be it the dope (coke or meth) in liquid form or the use of sophisticated hidden compartments. The places where things can be hidden and places that can be modified to conceal drugs are limitless with these folks. Then you wonder about what happens when the dope car gets to its destination. So, the driver is often told to leave the car at a public location and walk away. He gets a call when the car is back where he dropped it off. So, he has no clue what happens. Spending so many years debriefing smugglers gave me the ability to see things from their perspective. This is why, based on what the roadside interview goes like, I can tell if there will be cooperation for a controlled delivery. If the guy doesn't know much about the process, he can't really put things in motion.

QUICK ACCESS COMPARTMENTS

The mid-level drivers almost operate the same when it comes to where they meet. Except, they are making their exchanges in public areas, and for that, they must have quick access compartments. These are hidden locations that are often operated electronically by actuators and hydraulic pistons. I've even seen trunk latches used to hold a seat down, where the floor had been lowered to create the compartment. A push of a couple of buttons and the seat would raise up. This is made this way so that the wholesale mid-level buyer can give the cash to the high-level supplier and immediately hide the product and leave. It's the same concept as the BBQ shop owner having to pay Sam's Club or Costco for the ten briskets that he purchases to cook and sell at his store. There's an actual exchange. You ask why a public place? Because who would look at two guys sitting in a car for a minute and getting out with shopping bags in a mall parking as being suspicious? It's what happens in those parking lots. Remember, in plain sight and "Nothing is ever what it seems."

SUSPICIOUS ROUTE

I remember back in 2007, I stopped a guy in Mississippi who was coming from Laredo and heading to Chicago. The first thing I thought was, "What the hell is he doing in Mississippi?" In addition to lies and a slew of other tradecraft factors, I wanted to know why he had chosen this route and whose car he was driving. He was driving a Chrysler 300 with temporary Texas plates but handed me an Illinois driver's license. When I asked him about the ownership of the car, where he was headed, and why he was in MS, he told me it was his uncle's car. Now, let's forget about what makes sense and actually approach this with the mindset of "Why?" So, when he told me it was his uncle's car, he showed me some behaviors that made me think he was lying about the relationship aspect and was trying to make his story sound legit. He had a hard time explaining who the uncle was by name and how the hell his uncle had a Texas-plated car when he was supposedly living in Chicago.

Earlier, he mentioned he had flown with his uncle from Chicago to Laredo so that he could give his uncle a ride to the border so that his uncle could go to Mexico, and then instead of driving back, he said he wanted to drive his uncle's car back to his house in Chicago. WOW! You're probably amazed too. I know, it sounds all kinds of fishy! Wait, let me tell you what the reality was at the time.

After I found 66 pounds of Cocaine in a secondary floor that had been added to the trunk, I had a chance to debrief the guy. He was a mule for a high-level smuggling DTO, and we'll call him Jose for this book. So, Jose had been recruited by the Sinaloa Cartel because he had lost his oil field job in South Texas. Yes, his whole family was living in Chicago, and he had been working in South Texas for some time in the oil field.

The main reason he said he was recruited was because he had a license and no arrest record. The truth is, contrary to popular belief, high-level DTOs want drivers who have clean records. Because they know the last thing they need is a driver with a criminal history for drugs being stopped by the police. So, they offer the guy $20K to fly to Laredo and pick up this car to drive back to Chicago. In the process, Jose had to come up with some story as to what was going on and why he was driving to Chicago.

Now, as far as why he was all the way in Mississippi? He was told to go to Houston, take Interstate 10 to New Orleans, and then go up through Mississippi by turning on Interstate 59 and then up Interstate 65 to Gary, Indiana, where he would then be close to Chicago. Why all this way when he could have driven up I-35 to Dallas, then I-30 through Little Rock, Arkansas to I-40, and then to West Memphis, Arkansas, where he could have picked up I-55 and went straight up to Chicago?

The reason was that the cartel knew that I-35 between Waco and Dallas, I-30 between Dallas and Little Rock, and I-55 in Illinois had proven problematic for them in the past. This specific group, according to Jose, had lost over ten loads over the last few years to interdiction officers in these areas. Now, obviously, adjustments had to be made to maintain its clandestine operational security and asset management. As you can tell by now, what I talked about previously about being given directions and routes was also present in this scenario. These are all elements of high-level DTO tradecraft leaking throughout the interview and debriefs.

No Tools in a Work Truck

Summer of 2009, I stopped a flatbed work truck that had small signs on the doors. The one-ton pickup truck was registered to a guy in Miami and was clean. Just washed and the tires had enough shine on them, you would have thought this eight-year-old truck had just been driven off the showroom floor at the dealership. What I noticed as I walked up to the passenger side was that there were no tools for any trade, and no scratches on the bed. Looked a bit odd for a work truck, but I figured maybe the guy was proud of it, as most new truck owners are. I say new, because the truck had just been purchased not even a month ago.

I spoke to the driver, standing on the right side of the truck (we do this, so we don't get run over by a passing car) and noticed the guy was dressed as if he was going to a party. He was wearing really expensive shoes, which cost about one mortgage payment for my house now and he had one little backpack in the front seat. This pickup was a single cab and I couldn't see any other luggage. All fine and dandy, until we ended up talking about his journey.

So, this fella, who was headed to California, was apparently job searching and he had decided to just make a drive out to Cali for a month and see if he could land a job. Of course, he had no clue what part and couldn't decide if he wanted to go to Los Angeles or the Bay Area. What he did tell me was that he had a buddy that he would call when he got to Los Angeles. As mentioned before the DTOs compartmentalize components of the operation. This is a huge sign of clandestine activity and one of the most common areas, where the mules fail. You see, the cartel can't afford a mule to get stopped, arrested, and then cooperate. That would mean they could make the delivery under the supervision of the police and the rest of the cartel's staff and operation would be jeopardized.

If you think about the Osama Bin Laden (OBL) Raid that the SEALs conducted in 2011, there were over 400 personnel assigned to that mission. But, knowing the way the CIA and the DOD operate, you can rest assured that only a small handful of folks in that entire process knew who the target was and what they were working on. If you watched any of the movies they've made about it, you will see that even the SEAL Team that was responsible for the operation did not know for a fact about OBL, until the night they were deploying. This is exactly the purpose of compartmentalization.

If a small component is compromised, the entire mission is not jeopardized. The mission will continue, and another person is plugged into that slot. But, in the event there are any leaks, the damage is minimal, because that person only knows a small portion of what they are doing and only what they are to do. Most of the time in missions they don't even know the direction they are headed. The same goes with cartels not telling all the details to their load drivers, so the smuggling operations have some level of management and information is limited to minimize exploiting the operation.

After a few minutes of speaking to the driver of the flatbed and picking up on a slew of other factors associated with clandestine activity, I got permission to search the truck and found a secret compartment that was built between the two frame rails of the flatbed pickup, inside containing over $200K in US Currency that was all heat sealed and wrapped in axle grease and mustard. Why do you ask? I guess the cartel thinks the drug dogs won't smell the dope that is on the money. You ask: "Dope on the money?" Yes! They use the same facilities to count and package money and place them in the same hidden compartments. This compartment had obviously been used for many years, since the inside was all rusted and the screw holes that held the door in place were all scratched up and looked used and abused.

I obviously won't go into details about all the factors that we look for but let's just say that there are hundreds if not thousands of variations of them and they change from encounter to encounter. Just as do the mules. They have mules who are teenagers, older grandpas and grandmas in RVs and even gay/lesbian couples with their dogs. The reality is all living people like money and there is a ton of money to be made by smuggling. As long as there is a demand, there will be a supply of it and mules are going to get paid for the drives. It is the name of the game and they all have tradecraft components that they leak for the most part through communication.

WHY?

As time went on in my career and I started to debrief more and more of my crooks, I went back and studied my old case files from the late 90's, early 2000's and even videos of cars that I had searched and hadn't found anything. I ran the car license plates, watched the videos and started dissecting the interviews in a different manner. I took the approach of asking myself that simple question "WHY?" again. The simplest yet most powerful question of all time. That three-letter word can expose so much!

I applied it to the videos I reviewed as I watched their demeanors and listened to the responses, trying to figure out what it was that they were trying to convince me to be the truth. Because if I can nail that, I can expose the truth! Now, folks lie, and they lie all the time for a multitude of reasons. They lie because they worry about status and what they are projected as being, they lie to minimize an offense like speeding in hopes of not getting a ticket, they lie to cover up the fact that they are illegally in the U.S., they even lie, when they are on the way to cheat on their spouse, and so many other reasons. As interdiction officers, we hear lies day in and day out. But, knowing the tradecraft and knowing how to determine if the lies are intended to cover up some sort of operation itself becomes the challenge.

What I want to clarify here is that there are no standards as to the type of lies you will get or specific things to look for that is universally applied to discover clandestine activity. You just simply have to understand that an operation consists of many components and a legitimate business, a legitimate traveler, or a legitimate worker will have no reason to hide specifics. Unless, they are involved in an operation that is totally illegal, immoral, or projects a negative perception on those engaged in doing it. Of course, criminals do travel and they all will lie, but how would you be able to determine the smuggler out of the bunch and what is it that you are supposed to look for?

It is an ever-changing process and as technology becomes more advanced and the more advanced the world gets; the more tactics are employed to help in the process of maintaining clandestine components. I mean, who would have thought they would pay for thousands of kilos of Cocaine by Bitcoin Transfers from Europe? Smugglers aren't stupid. It is a 150-billion-dollar annual worldwide industry. They have better equipment than most police forces around the globe!

ALL GOOD THINGS COME TO AN END

That late night in October 2009, when I had stopped JC, I had walked up to the back of the car, and before I made it up there, JC yelled out of the window: "I got a dog in here!" I stop dead in my tracks, not knowing if it's a vicious dog or not. The last thing I want to do is have to shoot a man's dog. So, I asked him to exit the car and meet me in the back. JC jumps out of the car, and I can tell by his strut towards the back that he's excited and the adrenaline is flowing.

It's pretty normal to see this during the first contact with any driver. What happens when the lights come on is the person driving experiences fear, and a burst of epinephrine is released into the brain. It triggers all kinds of reactions, which are the same components a polygraph test measures. One of them is the burst of energy and elevated heart rate. So, JC walks over to the back and immediately starts to take over the conversation. An Alpha by nature and now under the influence of adrenalin, it's his natural reaction to take charge. What I don't know at this point is that he's actually freaking out.

Remember I said he had military orders? Well, he did, and his CAC card. CAC is the military ID card that all service members carry to get into the base and other various facilities. But the orders and the CAC card were in the same bag with the money, so the whole cover story he had used for nearly a decade is about to come unraveled in his mind. He knows he can't retrieve either one of the two tangible items he needs to convince me of his cover because as soon as he would open the backpack, I would see the two large heat-sealed packages of US Currency in the same bag.

All he had in the bag was the two large bundles, his dog leash, his CAC card, and his travel orders. That one JanSport bag was the end of his career as a smuggler. According to him, it was the best thing that happened to him, and he's grateful it happened. He has a young son now, and his focus is to make sure his kid doesn't get involved in criminal activity.

As I explained to JC the reason for the stop, he was so excited he started to use a lot of verbal and non-verbal responses that seemed very exaggerated, and his answers weren't even making sense. I told him I stopped him for not using his signals, and he replied: "I used my signal when I went around you, and I'm sorry about that!" Made no sense. But, having that adrenalin dump into the system obviously affects the motion of the neurotransmitters and the small pulses that carry the data in the brain. No worries, we move on to the next topics.

FIVE MAIN TOPICS VS. INDICATORS

When engaging folks in general conversation, we focus on five (5) main topics. These are topics that are extensively covered in our courses and in the *Evading Honesty®* book. So, I won't go much into reprinting the same material here, but I'll highlight the main concept.

Everyone who is traveling has five basic elements in common. These are Origin, Destination, Purpose, Length, and Relationships. Some are at face value and understandable by you as the reader, except the last two. By length, I refer to the length of time that the trip is supposed to take. No matter what the age, gender, lifestyle or race, everyone who travels will have a length of time in mind as to the duration of their journey. That is from start to finish. This means if someone is off a week and is on vacation, they will respond within *a week* if asked about the length of time.

The relationships aspect is a bit tricky because it has many components. That could be passengers in the car, who they visited, are going to visit, the owner of the car, the insured, and so on. Basically, anyone who has ties to either what's in the car, the car itself, or anyone encountered during this specific journey.

With those in mind, we have to also realize that unless someone is worried about perception and may be involved in immoral activity like infidelity, almost all people who are stopped by the police will have no reason to minimize, influence the perception of, or outright lie to the police about any of those components. However, a smuggler has to lie about the whole entire process. Remember, they are smuggling, and that is the only reason they are on the road. Hence, they rely on a cover story to convince.

As I started to write JC a warning, I engaged him in other conversations surrounding his itinerary. So, in essence, the five elements mentioned above became the topic. JC, who by now you know is a professional smuggler with tenure under his belt, is supposed to have his shit together. Or you would think. But he falls apart. I ask him where he's headed, and he replies, "I'm coming from Baton Rouge, visiting my folks, and now I'm headed back to California," as he shifts his weight and starts pointing out west toward the direction of California. Now remember that I have stopped him on Interstate 20 in Texas, about an hour and a half east of Dallas, and he is driving west. As a reader or if you're listening to the audiobook, you may think to yourself, "What is wrong with what he said?" To the untrained ear and untrained eye, the responses seem convincing. Remember, the behavior is manifesting and the story-line of the cover, and how the brain reacts when fear sets in.

The reality is every single thing JC did was throwing up red flags. First off, I asked him about the destination, and he went back, started with the origin, then the purpose, and then arrived at the answer. This indicated several things. One being he was telling me the story he had rehearsed. As mentioned, now we know he was actually coming from New Orleans, but he said Baton Rouge. I didn't know about New Orleans until later that night when he was cooperating, but from the way he spilled his rehearsed (cover) story and went on to answer the origin, destination, and purpose without being asked and the fact that his body language changed and he went into illustration mode with his pointing at the direction, he essentially exhibited signs of fear.

The adrenalin dump hit, and his short-term memory was about to dissipate. He had practiced his story about the five elements, leaving out New Orleans and using a less likely city that drugs would be transported to, and he also knew that he couldn't use his cover of being on a recruiting mission anymore. Why? Remember? His orders are in that bag with the cash from the delivery of 200 pounds of weed. So, his demeanor is telling on him, and he is trying his hardest to appear normal and convincing.

I can go on and on about the various behaviors he exhibited, and what you will find is that the same factors are being exhibited showing his deception, the same tradecraft markers are shown as he attempts to maintain certain clandestine components of his story and overall, he fails miserably. The reason for that is that the subconscious always knows the truth, and it will always create conflict when a human attempts to be deceptive. And remember, JC was a special case. He was not only a professional, he also had extensive training in operating in a clandestine manner in the armed forces and even more by working for the cartel.

This is why in my classes, also called **Smugglers, Inc.®**, I focus on these elements rather than superficial common denominators that are commonly referred to as *Indicators*. I don't even like that term. It has a certain level of presumptive notion to it as if a single thing can be 100% indicative of smuggling, other than just seeing a bundle of dope in the front seat of a car as the officer walks up to the passenger side door.

The cover story JC used was that he had gone to Baton Rouge for a couple of days to see his relatives, who he had not seen since Hurricane Katrina hit back in 2005. Remember, he was attempting to change my perception, but he was unable to control his reactions. The behaviors and tradecraft exhibited are what made him get caught.

JC HELPS OUT

A few years later, JC called me and asked if I would like for him to come to some of my classes and talk to the students learning this craft. He wanted to help, and we have fun doing it, even now. But before he decided to do that, we went over the video. JC was amazed at how much he blew the interview and could not believe his reactions. He admitted many times in the class and in person to me and others that he had practiced so much and, in his mind, he was doing a good job, but the two components that I teach to help identify are literally the two components that he leaked out unknowingly.

JC reviewed the video several times and even used it to explain numerous times to the students what was going through his mind when I would ask a question. He admits that no matter how much he practiced and had mastered the craft on his end, he had never encountered a situation like when he and I met that night in 2009. He and I did a recording for a class in July of 2019, where he tells the students in the class that after the first four minutes of the nearly fourteen-minute stop that night, he knew he was screwed, and after that, all he did was try to change my perception. The funny thing is, I wasn't questioning him at all about his responses, just simply asking him about the five elements and the stress it was causing him, which made him lose control of his cover story.

Essentially it boils down to the fact that no matter how prepared anyone is, when they are lying, it is about questioning the motive and not the lie itself that will reveal the truth and exhibit the behaviors and responses someone looks for, not the attempt to make sense of the situation and story. Anyone can come up with a plausible response and make it appear to make sense. The reality is, what makes sense to one person, makes no sense to another. Case and point, the drive to attend the Quinceañera mentioned previously.

PART TWO
THE CHASE

FALSE IMPRESSIONS

When we get into the law enforcement side and the efforts to identify and apprehend smugglers, we run into some unique challenges. One of the main challenges is the lack of training or the inadequate levels that exist. Over the last several decades, mainstream law enforcement training has taken on the culture of relying on statistical data and sometimes even no applicable methodologies to identify the criminal minds.

No Two People Will Respond the Same

The number of training courses that focus on statistical data to come up with ways to identify criminal activity is astonishing. It's as if we have taken the science of mathematics and the results of analytical research based on an algorithm of numbers and possibilities to find quick references to identification. As a human being, I personally have a hard time processing how the science of numbers and mathematics are applied to a situation where behaviors and moral issues are the driving factors behind actions, responses, and demeanors. Any psychologist will tell you that no two people will react the same to every situation, and no two people will respond the same way to stress caused by fear. So, to apply a set of standardized indicators as to what to physically look for in a person is literally faulty at its core.

An example is the old saying, "If they don't look at you, then they're lying!" The reality is this is one of those reactions that can no doubt be attributed to deception, but what if it's culturally motivated? In some cultures, the presence of a person with a position of authority can affect one's responses. In some cultures, the age of the interviewer can affect the responses, and, in some cultures, the fact that the interviewer may be of the opposite sex can and will affect the interviewee's eye contact.

So, What do Officers Need to Focus On?

So, what do officers need to focus on when considering the lies and how to detect them? The first step is to get training. Those who are experts in identifying and apprehending smugglers have thousands of hours of training and a lot of trial and error experience. At the same time, those who work interdiction also know the difference between the lies themselves and the motivating factors of those lies. This means rather than focusing on algorithms of common demeanors applied across the board, these select few know how to formulate the right questions at the right time and will know, based on their expertise, if they're being lied to. We spoke about clandestine activities and how smugglers must work under the radar, often posing as something they're not. The same goes for how they reply to simple questions about the elements they must lie about. Those were: Origin, Destination, Purpose, Length, and Relationships.

Remembering that smugglers are attempting to maintain a clandestine level is essential in how to analyze the behaviors and correctly categorize the encounter. Reactions can be manifested in various ways. And the officer must be able to decipher through the conscious and subconscious responses that are exhibited and then be able to categorize the responses to recognize what type of clandestine activity is happening and then narrow it down to smuggling activity. Every criminal action comes with a set of specific tradecraft markers. Sure, some call it a profile, but we're not talking about a profile of a person but an action. In this case, it's smuggling. In the spy world, they call this Spycraft. Tradecraft of spies is essentially what that means.

At the end of the day, to a smuggler, there must be a cover action and cover story to make it look legitimate. That is how someone is identified. If I go to visit my sister in Birmingham, Alabama, I don't have to have a cover story to tell an officer if I'm stopped along the way and I won't be exhibiting behaviors associated with fear. (Unless I'm scared of getting a ticket for hauling ass. Ha!) But, once I know the outcome, my fear is no longer an issue, because the consequence is known. Either a warning or a ticket. That's all! Now, if a person is smuggling cocaine, would he/she really be worried about the warning or the ticket? Obviously, the consequence of being caught with the cocaine would be far greater and more inclined to include prison time, so the more the motivation to lie, be nervous, and attempt to change the perception of the officer stopping the person. And what better way than to have a cover story and lie to convince the officer of the fallacy!

By now, you may be wondering about the safety of the officers when it comes to the violence that goes with the drug trafficking world. The reality is, smugglers come in various levels of operation. The driving factor behind all smuggling operations is obviously the greed for money. Keeping that in mind, we must also consider the culture of each level. The higher level, which would be the ones that would be smuggling 50 kilograms of cocaine are part of a larger, transnational smuggling operation that value their operational security more than a single load being lost. One of the ways is to *not* attract the heat from the law enforcement and government entities worldwide. I mean, think about it: Why would El Chapo's (Sinaloa Cartel) organization member want to get in a shoot-out with a trooper on the side of the road in West Texas and have the wrath of Texas and Federal Law Enforcement on them?

In case you didn't know, one of those cartels kidnapped a DEA agent in Guadalajara, Mexico in the 80's, tortured, and killed him. And boy, was it a bad move for that cartel at the time. The wrath of the DEA, and a lot of other three letter agencies including the Langley bunch came down on the cartel so hard, they gave up the guy responsible. Why? They have a business to run and scrutiny leads to losses.

Talking about losses, I get asked all the time: "Shawn, you've been catching smugglers for a quarter of a century, sent a lot of them to prison and have seized a lot of their assets. So, do you not worry about them coming to kill you?" Collectively, we're talking about upwards of thirty million dollars in cash and other tangible assets they're referring to by making that statement. But I don't worry about the retaliation. I'll explain the reason coming up next.

I Don't Worry About Retaliation

I've been fortunate enough to work with some of the bad asses that do the same work I do, and my success is partially credited to the groups I've worked with as team members. I'm not going to disclose personal stats, but I'll tell you that it's a pretty good chunk of what was mentioned. It's not really about the numbers with the job, but the mission itself. Back to the original question about being concerned, the reality is that the cartel or any organized criminal enterprise is a business and every business, legit or illegal, expects to have losses. Seizures of their product and proceeds is just a part of the game. They simply ensure they don't have leaks.

So, are they concerned with me or any other officer? No, they know losses are part of the business. Now, what about those dirty cops who steal from the cartel? That's another story! They're targets for sure. There's a level of mutual respect that exists. One plays a mouse and the other plays a cat; it's the chase and it's like a game of catching, as long as no one oversteps their boundaries. And, in this case, boundaries often look like a dirty cop stealing from the cartel or the cartel members killing legit cops stateside. We already covered what happens to those who hurt cops from the USA side. (The DEA agent in Guadalajara, Mexico in the 80's). Dirty cops? Oh, they're real and sometimes we see news blurbs of some cop somewhere being kidnapped and hurt, having his fingers cut off and then dumped somewhere. But the details always seem to fade away with time and no one is captured to be punished for it. The truth always prevails on the law enforcement side.

Let's talk about the risk management efforts and the misunderstanding that exists stateside by officers. Remember the part about cover stories and thinking about what to say if they get stopped. This is a common thing amongst smuggling organizations. They learn what officers look for and counter it.

Back in the mid 80's, until even today, there are classes that teach officers to look for certain physical characteristics to identify a smuggler. These range from air fresheners, to how much luggage, the appearance of the interior as if someone has been driving a long way to even the color of the car, stickers, and even shit that has no relevance to criminal activity like Catholic Rosary Beads and Virgin the Guadalupe. These are all common denominators I was referring to earlier. We all know that none of this stuff is exclusively related to smuggling. I mean shit folks, while we're at it, why not throw in the use of shirts, pants, shoes, and oxygen. Don't smugglers use them when smuggling too? Hence, my efforts to show that tradecraft, clandestine activity, and deception are what sets aside the law-abiding general public from the criminal who travels the roads.

Either way, when these things are listed in a police report, the cartel uses assets management and protection tactics to counter them, now that they know. So, they remove these elements as time goes on to minimize being categorized and, in their mind, targeted. You see, it's not as simple as some think. And cartels aren't stupid, unlike the stupid hoodrat who sells baggies of weed on your neighborhood street corner, toting a cheap ass gun, in fear he's going to be shot in an exchange with a gangbanger or user.

THERE'S NO STANDARD TO HOW CLANDESTINE ACTIVITY IS CONDUCTED

One thing for sure is that by this point in this book, you've realized that there is no chronological order in which this book is written and there's no rhyme or rhythm to what is being said. There's a reason for that and that's because catching smugglers doesn't come with a set of standard applications that officers should learn and apply. There's no standard to how clandestine activity is conducted, how tradecraft is applied and how a person lies, affecting their responses and the detection of all these factors. So, in essence, it's like life itself. You use your imagination and drive, set goals, and accomplish them based on what is normal to you. Smugglers do the same. Except their life is facade. But, if you know the big picture, then you can put the pieces of the puzzle together, by knowing what pieces fit and what pieces don't.

We have to learn that applying the linear learning, communicating, and application of standards to a non-linear situation, which changes by time and location, cannot be effective. Just as much as writing this book in a linear format is not going to be triggering your imagination of the complexity of smuggling operations and the intellect it takes to play the game as an interdiction officer. The next time you see those special looking police cars parked in the median on a rural highway, you'll be reminded that even though it looks like they're just sitting there, they're really engaged in one of the most complex enforcement actions known in the law enforcement community. "Nothing is ever what it seems!"

As a civilian member of the public, you should be getting the idea that smugglers aren't caught just by accident. As an officer learning about interdiction, you should be noticing that working counter-smuggling on the rural highways or streets is not the same as catching a person who is drunk and applying the standardization of the field sobriety tests. As a prosecutor, you should be realizing that to get the testimony on record, it takes more than just quick questions to get a single point on record. And finally, if you're a smuggler, you should know that your attempts to maintain a clandestine operation will fail when you're stopped by one of the officers who specializes in detecting clandestine activity and no matter how much you practice, you can't control your response. But hey, thanks for buying the book! Ha!

THE GAVEL

The power of the gavel, having slammed against the sound block resting on the judge's bench, rings through the years served in prison by the smugglers. This small wooden tool is used by judges to set the rules, decisions, and punishments for smugglers. However, behind it is a comprehensive methodology used to determine facts and conjecture. For the road officer, meeting the elements of the crime establishes the charges, but in the smuggling world, seldom are the elements met easily. Remember that smugglers operate in a clandestine manner, so the chances of just seeing their drugs in plain sight are hardly the case. When an officer makes a traffic stop, he has certain rules to abide by. There are constitutional rights, laws that define the crimes, and of course, agency policies that may or may not restrict their actions.

We see a headline that says: "Man arrested by

troopers for having 25 pounds of heroin after he allows officers to search his truck!" and some think to themselves: "Wow! That was stupid! Why would he let the cops search him?" The reality is that the smuggler is either hoping the officer won't search the car, or if he searches the car, he won't find the hidden compartment that holds the drugs, or he simply just gives up, knowing his number was pulled. Smugglers aren't just single-time smugglers for quick cash. The greed of easily making thousands of dollars keeps them running loads, and eventually, they're going to end their streak. Their fear is not necessarily the cops or even jail time but losing a load worth millions of dollars and having to pay it back to the owner. They're not only legally responsible for the punishment from the government if they get caught, but they're also responsible for losing the organization's assets. Either way, there's a gavel that will slam the tabletop. They would rather it be the gavel in a courtroom than the gavel that marks the end of their life by the cartel owners of the drugs.

Cops have to rely on legal things to do their work, while the cartels have no legal system. It's more of an asset management effort. Their asset management style changes from group to group and the person who commits the violation. When it comes to cops, they even have to rely on explanations to justify their actions because that gavel is blind. It also represents the system that affords the occupants of the land the ability to challenge the charges. To justify the extension of a traffic stop to something more, cops must rely on what is referred to as reasonable suspicion. That's being able to articulate what they have encountered and, based on their training and tenure, convince the jurors or the judge why they didn't do it in a specific time frame because a traffic stop is a temporary detention and falls under search and seizure guidelines of the US Constitution. To make things even more difficult, sometimes they must rely on factors that alone could be innocent, but the manner that they are related to a specific crime would show their correlation to a criminal act. This is where that training and experience comes in.

VOLUNTARY CONSENT TO SEARCH

It's true that any officer can just ask to search a car–it's called voluntary consent to search. Which means an officer just asks the person straight forward. That's it! It's that simple! Most folks will simply allow it unless they're concerned with something being broken during the search or they've had negative experiences with cops. And lastly, sometimes a smuggler will allow it to show less suspicion. I know this first hand because I have been a victim of the last part.

I used to think that if someone was hauling dope or money, they would never just say I could search. But then I popped a few people with loads just sitting in the trunk and asked them why they volunteered consent to search. They all said that they were told to be cooperative and that most cops wouldn't search them. When I was a rookie, I used to see cops on traffic stops ask folks to search, and when they said okay, they would let them go and not do the search. When I asked them why, the typical answer would be something like, "Well, dude, if they had anything, they wouldn't be so open and allow you to search." Of course, for the last quarter of a century, I've had less than ten people tell me "No!" and all but one only had personal use drugs!

THE LAW

We have to also think about other things like case law. The US criminal justice system is broken down into so many jurisdictions that not every place works the same. You can be in one state, and as long as you operate within the confines of the US Constitution and the agency policy, you can pretty much do anything. And in some states, the higher courts, as in Appellate and State Supreme Courts, can rule a specific opinion that restricts an officer. But that type of case law only applies in that jurisdiction.

The difference between law and case law, for those who don't know, is that one is drafted, voted on, and put into law by lawmakers at the local, state, and federal level. While case law is an opinion handed down by a court that interprets gray areas and simply by published opinions, things can change and get affected. And sometimes, it makes certain local, state, and federal laws more restrictive. It's a complicated realm of the criminal justice system, for sure; but officers must keep in mind that their area is affected by the courts that have jurisdiction over the area they operate in. The only court in the United States that has overall jurisdiction and its opinions affect everyone across the board is the United States Supreme Court.

All that case law stuff aside, there are certain rules in place when it comes to making interdiction stops. First and foremost, there must be probable cause or reasonable suspicion, which are dictated by the enforcement type. A police officer, deputy sheriff, or anyone who works for a local, county, state, or even some federal agency must have probable cause for a traffic stop.

REASONABLE SUSPICION VS MERE SUSPICION

In certain areas like the buffer zones near the US/International Borders, certain other factors are considered. We'll look at US Border Patrol (USBP) instead. They have Immigration Checkpoints within a certain area of the borderline, where everyone must stop. Surely some folks think this is illegal, but it is also safety and security that enables this act to take place. Within those areas, the chances of an illegal alien being present in a car is higher than, let's say, on Interstate 80 in Nebraska. The USBP also doesn't necessarily have to have probable cause for their roving units to make traffic stops, but rather *Mere Suspicion*. The threshold for *Reasonable* and *Mere Suspicion* is different. *Mere Suspicion* takes much less to articulate, while

Reasonable Suspicion is what an entire interdiction stop is all about.

In Layman's Terms, *Reasonable Suspicion* is often referred to as factors that the officer can articulate in a manner that would show, based on his training and experience, something is fishy as compared to other situations he has encountered. This could be established on an interdiction stop by articulating specific components of observed tradecraft, as mentioned previously, and behaviors associated with being deceptive, which collectively would mount to the suspicion that clandestine activity is happening at that time.

Remember that smugglers must operate in a clandestine manner to avoid being detected. I used the word *Collectively* for a reason. It's synonymous with the term *Totality of Circumstances*, which is the legal term for the entire big picture. So, the presence of all factors associated with clandestine activity, depicted by the tradecraft markers and the behaviors showing that the person is lying, will establish reasonable suspicion. The general opinion of the courts is that if an officer can explain something is wrong, he/she is justified in extending that original detention and investigating further. This is also the same concept used to justify detention in the event a police dog must be summoned to sniff around a car.

As mentioned, the way this legal stuff works is complex, and it's so broad it is discussed over a 3-year graduate-level educational facility we all know as law school. And the fact that it changes from place to place, it's worthless to attempt to speak of what is applicable now because next year or sometime in the future, it is subject to change. So, if you're a member of the general public reading this, please remember that the dynamic nature of the laws and opinions in court is so different when you read an article that seems odd as to the way it was handled as compared to your area, it could simply be the way that place works.

As an example, in some states, when an officer gets a K9 alert to a car, he must stop and take the car to the office, and draw an affidavit to have a judge issue a search warrant before the search is conducted. But, in other states, an officer can have probable cause on the scene and doesn't need a search warrant. And to take it further, in some areas, there are case laws in place that give an officer probable cause just based on the factors, which in other states would only mount to suspicion. So, nothing with legal stuff is standard across the board, just as there are no standards as to the level of operations, tradecraft of maintaining a clandestine operation, and how folks respond to the fear of being caught when they lie.

SMUGGLERS DO NOT FIT THE STANDARD MOLD

Everyone acts and does things differently; hence it's imperative for the officers to be well-rounded. Interdiction and intercepting smugglers is not as simple as writing a speeding ticket or even arresting someone for being drunk. It's extremely complex and has a lot of moving parts. Speaking of drunks, did you know the fact that the tests are standardized makes their application and outcome standard across the board all over North America? Totally the opposite of how smugglers are caught.

While we are on the topic of standardization, we also need to understand that officers must not have the mindset that interdiction stops, or smugglers fit some sort of standard mold. This is where officers make the biggest mistakes. They look for common denominators and attempt to make things be there when they're not, and when it comes to explanations or testimony, they end up getting hammered by the defense lawyers. Remember the eye contact issue? How is it not across the board applicable to everyone? And if you're a civilian reading this, I'm pretty sure you wouldn't want to be compared to anyone else either. It takes your individuality away!

The Workups and Counter-Measures

The counter to smuggling is the interdiction efforts of law enforcement worldwide. These efforts start at the international level and work their way down to the local level in every country. The CIA collects intelligence, sometimes passing it along to the Federal Law Enforcement counterparts stateside and even the attaché offices at US Embassies around the globe. I'm talking about the DEA, US Customs, and so on. Most of their work requires long-term surveillance and coordination with various other international and stateside federal agencies to stop the flow of drugs/money. But at the state and local levels, the enforcement is left to the local police or sheriff and, at times, the state police agencies. Within these realms is where you find the interdiction efforts on the highways. Selecting the right personnel for these units has its own criteria that are not known by many administrators.

Selecting the right person is key to the success of the unit/team. DELTA Force, SEALs, Air Force Paratroopers, and Marine Corps Special Operations (MARSOC) all have selection processes to weed out the ones who don't possess the well-rounded candidate needed. This is the most crucial decision an administrator must make. It can literally make or break the purpose and outcome! We already discussed the complexity of smuggling operations in the first part of this book. Now, we have to look at what it is that these interdiction officers must possess.

CRITERIA FOR INTERDICTION OFFICERS

In any kind of work that requires engagement with various cultures and demographics, the engaging person must possess an open mind. This means he/she can't have limitations in understanding and communication skills. We all know of that one person who is simply socially awkward, and either has no personality or an overbearing one to the point that he/she offends anyone who is engaged in simple conversations. Imagine being engaged with someone who is dry, to the point, and displays no emotions, nor do they display any empathy. It would make for an uncomfortable scene and, certainly, no ability to continue a meaningful conversation.

So, whoever is to be selected for an interdiction position should, at the very least, be able to have a basic conversation with just about anyone about any topic and should be able to do so without being confrontational. The stereotypical perception amongst the public is that when being engaged by law enforcement, it's like speaking to a character resembling Joe Friday and hearing the words "Just the Facts, Ma'am!" But in reality, an interdiction officer needs to possess a pleasant personality and be witty.

A non-judgmental, non-opinionated approach to new conversations is the way to open the door to communication. This means if you're an administrator or a supervisor tasked with selecting the person, you want to choose the one who has an outgoing personality. This will not only help the engagements be smooth but also cuts down on complaints from those who may get offended if the officer has rough edges. Now, we're not talking about this as the only important trait, but it's the essential criterion. Without communication, there is no foundation to extract the tradecraft and recognize clandestine activity.

Drive! We call that the eagerness to accomplish a mission and doing it at all costs. The only problem is that this specific mission has to be conducted with consideration to civil rights afforded to all citizens and visitors regardless of legal status. Essentially, everyone has constitutional rights, and they must be protected, not you do what you want at whatever cost. Now, how do we select the driven ones? It's not about the one who writes the most tickets on patrol or the one who lifts the most weight. That might work for the SWAT operator position, but not this one all the time. Imagine a person who has the ability to think, foresee, and solve a problem before it even becomes one. Someone who can address it without any reservation, with perfection, and then refocus back on the original mission. That is what we are looking for.

Confidence is key, and thinking on your feet is a must. However, the desire for accolades is problematic as it drives the person to compete with others, and when the mission is failing, corners are cut to give the appearance that things are done correctly. But, contrary to appearance, it's a liability at all levels. As a civilian, you're reading this and thinking to yourself, "Don't all officers have to pass a psychological test?" The reality is that in this job, some do fall through the cracks. The system is not foolproof. As a supervisor, you are thinking, "How do I ensure the liability doesn't fall back on me?"

WHAT A SUPERVISOR SHOULD LOOK FOR

That's an excellent question, and here are some suggestions:

1. **Make sure you select the person who wants to do this for the right reasons.**
   That would be for the purpose of contributing to society. Not for notoriety, accolades, or even a confidence booster.
   These are compensation techniques used to

fulfill the lack of confidence. You don't want any part of that kind of officer.

2. **Invest in the training.** I know, I know! Budgets are an issue, but if you want a specialized unit with special skills, you must invest in a lot of special training and equipment. I don't see a SWAT team just throwing folks on the team and not giving them the training they need. Not only do they get extensive tactical training, they also get a lot of equipment to do their job. Interdiction is no different. So, when your guy/gal says, "I need a scope, tools, lift, and even a portable X-Ray machine…" it's not for looks. It really takes these items to find those high-level compartments.

3. **Let's not forget psychological pressure.** Remember when I said about the *Drive*? That means the person is self-driven. Like a lion that hunts and doesn't stop until the prey is captured. There's no need to push the lion. It's a genetic feature of the hunter. The last thing the lion needs is cheering. He's already programmed to hunt. You just have to let it go and give it the terrain to hunt on. That's how interdiction works. You don't pressure the person; you don't set goals because they already have them, and you don't restrict their movement. This means they operate the way they best see fit.

They use equipment they're given to use, and then they do what they are told at every level. Now, take that same concept and apply it to the Army's DELTA force. They're the masters of direct-action operations, and they work on their tactics every day. So, it becomes the result of the mission that the focus is placed on and not so much on the methodology deployed. They're told what is needed, and the guys themselves decide what route to take and how to get it done. They're given everything they could possibly need, and they're there's a lot of resources invested in their success. They get the mission done and only use their tactics, not orders. That's how it works! Silent, effective, and mission-oriented!

Remember accolades and notoriety? No one knows what a Delta or SEAL operator has done, and they don't advertise it. At least not until they're either out and in the limelight with a book or they're dead! That's when one finds out. That's the personality you want. The silent ones who focus on the mission, and you have to do your part to enable them to operate to their full potential. The last thing an administrator needs to do is to push for production. These guys are already maxed out on drive and eagerness. You don't need to shut them down. Discouraging your operators will result in losing them. I've seen many get burned out and leave the job because of the pressure put on them by their bosses to produce!

The Digital World

With technology ramping up and everything going digital, the tools available to law enforcement become more technical. We now have fiberoptic scopes and portable X-Ray machines that can be used to search cars. More advanced technology like Automatic License Plate Readers (ALPRs) are also everywhere, along with so many other small gadgets and technology tools that exist in the world. Because of the increase in technology, it's becoming more and more complex to identify smugglers. Meanwhile, smuggling organizations aren't ignorant in this regard; in fact, they know all about it. They use burner phones, as mentioned, so they don't leave traces. They know about ALPRs, and I have encountered those who have attempted to conceal their license plates, so there is no trace of their travel pattern. On top of that, civil rights organizations have attempted to curb the use of the ALPRs, citing privacy issues.

The reality is that ALPRs are like a set of eyes. When you, as a human being, look at a plate, you can see more than what an ALPR can see. That is the color of the car, the make and model, even who is driving it, and what race they are. While the ALPR simply captures the image and stores it. It doesn't know the owner, address, color, or any of the information you and any other person could see, as that same vehicle is observed by the naked eye. It's simply stored to see where that car was sighted previously.

What many don't know is that a good many of the international terrorism suspects are tracked that way. The FBI and other intelligence agencies identify the vehicles used by terrorists through other means and are able to locate them faster by checking the stored photos of the license plates. Unless they do an inquiry manually through the Department of Motor Vehicles, they would not know who the owner is, all they would know is where that car was seen. The same ALPRs are used by thousands of repossession companies to find the cars that have defaulted on their car loans and have repossession orders issued by the banks or dealerships who hold a lien on them.

Did you also know that the same ALPRs are responsible for tracking and alerting the police of assholes who had kidnapped kids and were headed to traffic them? Bank robbers have also been captured by the ALPR information, not to mention the number of stolen cars, Amber Alert victims, and Silver Alerts, which are old folks who have been lost while driving. So, when you hear the entities that claim this technology is tracking you, you can rest easy knowing no one tracks anyone unless the car is a suspect. I mean, when the systems nationwide are scanning and logging more than one billion tags a day, who has the time to look at all of them and wonder what movie theater you're going to? No one! No one really cares unless you're a child molester, terrorist, or a menace to society in a way that you must be apprehended before you kill or harm anyone.

TECHNOLOGY CAN BE USED FOR GOOD OR BAD

When it comes to the fast-growing availability of technological tools, law enforcement will be able to deploy tactics to help with the efforts to identify and apprehend the smugglers. But let's not forget that the same level of technology can and will help the smuggler maintain their cover. The use of secure chat apps like Facebook Secret Conversations, WhatsApp, and a slew of other communication methods with end-to-end encryption poses difficulties in conducting long-term surveillance of suspects. Not just smugglers but also terrorists, murderers, robbers, etc. Technology can be used for good and bad, as it doesn't measure and dictate its use based on morals. We must be cognizant of the fact that the introduction of any new tools has pros and cons related to case investigations.

Conclusion
At The End Of The Day

For centuries, products that have been deemed illegal by governments have been making it to the hands of the consumer. This is part of the supply and demand process. The more avenues that can be exploited will be considered, as the driving factor behind smuggling is gain, either financially or politically.

We must recognize the game of smuggling will never cease to exist, and it is far too complex to find a quick-witted solution that is effective. The mere dynamic nature of the ever-changing patterns and methodology makes combatting the craft extremely difficult. As we advance in this world, no matter the year, location, and the level of technology that is introduced, for the smuggling DTOs to maintain an effective operation, they must maintain a clandestine operation. As you have read, being clandestine in all aspects of the operations is literally the smuggler's best chance. This should be an indication that the dynamics will never change, and tradecraft recognition is the most effective way to analyze, identify, and apprehend the smuggling groups. It is my hope that by taking you through the journey into the world of smuggling, it helps those tasked with the identification and apprehension of the smugglers be able to see success and continue the efforts. Investing in one's self is the most important aspect of winning.

COMPLEX, CONTINUOUS TRAINING IS REQUIRED

As law enforcement officers, supervisors, and administrators reading this book, you must realize that the complexity of combatting the smuggling groups and their operational complexity requires continuous complex training. The fact that the operations aren't standard, the cookie-cutter, statistical-based approach to training and application is not effective and proves counterproductive. It wastes too many resources and a lot of energy spent by officers eager to work.

If you are a line officer, I suggest you invest in your training and ensure that you have reputable instructors. Don't limit your knowledge. "Education is the most powerful weapon you can use to change the world," is a quote by Nelson Mandela. Remember that and live by it. Seek the training you need to master this craft and don't rely on your employer or your peers to do it for you. Success comes from within, and you have to invest in your success. Seek, and you shall receive!

As a supervisor and administrator, if you are interested in starting or implementing a counter-smuggling or interdiction program, steps are taken to ensure proper funding for equipment and education and proper prosecution. The right investment in a business is the key to its success. No matter how anyone looks at it, specialized units are created for a purpose, which all boils down to the *return for investment* approach. So, select the right persons for the job and ensure they are provided with the training and tools to succeed.

If you are a prosecutor at any level, you must also ensure those caught smuggling get the highest and most deserving sentencing possible. This means you should also assist the agencies in investing in the training of their officers. As the person tasked with recording the testimony, I suggest you also familiarize yourself with the concepts here. The old ways of attempting to add up non-specific indicators and using the term *totality of circumstances* are no longer accepted in many courtrooms. Instead, the operational factors must be introduced to show the clandestine suspicions.

As a civilian reader, I hope you can now read those headlines and know that the warriors in those desolate lands are doing their best to keep you and your family safe. To extend a gesture of appreciation to them the next time you see them walking out of a store, eating at an establishment on duty, or just wave at them to let them know you thank them for their service.

And to my son Kamran, Baba Joon, by the time you are old enough to read and comprehend this book, I may or may not be around to joke about it with you.

But you have to know that this world exists in a way that any decision you make will affect your future. Always know that your actions affect you and those around you. Focus on always learning, serving mankind, and never taking time for granted. You will succeed at whatever you put your mind to, and I know you will make your Mom and me proud. Learn to be a good partner, husband, and father. You leave behind one thing that will always live on after you perish, and that is your legacy! I love you, son, and your mom loved you dearly!

"We'll be leaving together shortly!"
~ Shawn Pardazi

About the Author

With over 25 years of experience in civilian and federal law enforcement, Shawn has identified, apprehended, and debriefed hundreds of transnational smugglers. In his tenure, he successfully designed a system of properly identifying clandestine operations of smuggling groups by the deployment of tactics like those used by international intelligence agencies. The system, which includes the understanding of clandestine activity, tradecraft associated with its operational components, and how to extract human intelligence in face-to-face contacts, is described in this book, *Smugglers, Inc.*